Ladybugs

CLAIRE LLEWELLYN • BARRIE WATTS

W
FRANKLIN WATTS
A Division of Scholastic Inc.
NEW YORK TORONTO LONDON AUCKLAND SYDNEY
MEXICO CITY NEW DELHI HONG KONG
DANBURY, CONNECTICUT

First published in 2000 by Franklin Watts
96 Leonard Street, London EC2A 4XD

First American edition 2002 by Franklin Watts
A Division of Scholastic Inc.
90 Sherman Turnpike
Danbury, CT 06816

Series Editor: Anderley Moore
Editor: Rosalind Beckman
Series Designer: Jason Anscomb
Designer: Joelle Wheelwright
Illustrator: David Burroughs

Catalog details are available from the Library of Congress
Cataloging-in-Publication Data

ISBN 0-531-14654-5 (lib. bdg.) 0-531-14826-2 (pbk.)

Printed in China

Contents

What Are Ladybugs?

Ladybugs are small, round, brightly-colored beetles. Most of them are red or yellow with black spots. Some are brown or have different color spots, and a few have no spots at all.

▲ A 22-spot ladybug

▲ A 7-spot ladybug

▲ A 14-spot ladybug

Each kind of ladybug has its own pattern of spots.

Ladybugs belong to the insect family. Like all insects, they have three parts to their body: the head, the thorax, and the abdomen.

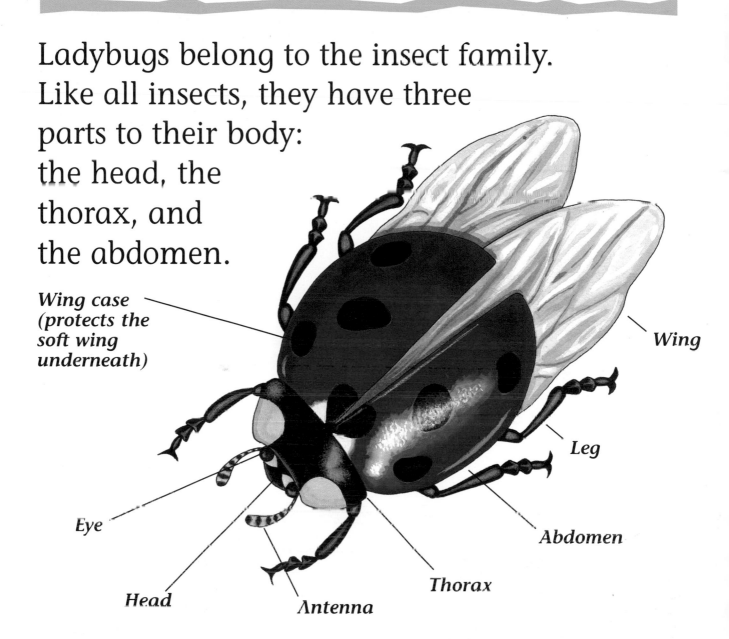

Wing case (protects the soft wing underneath)

Wing

Leg

Abdomen

Eye

Head

Antenna

Thorax

Ladybugs have three pairs of legs. All the parts of the body are covered in a tough case called the exoskeleton.

A ladybug uses its antennae to touch, taste, and smell things, and to pick up movements in the air.

A Ladybug's Food

Ladybugs are always hungry. They feed mostly on aphids. These are green, black, or white insects that crawl on roses and other plants.

Aphids are easy to catch because they move very slowly. Their soft, plump bodies are full of the juice they suck out of plants.

▲

Aphids feed on the sweet juice inside buds and stems.

Like many beetles, ladybugs have strong jaws for biting and chewing. They eat aphids and other tiny creatures very easily.

▲

A ladybug eats about a hundred aphids every day.

On the Wing

Ladybugs spend most of their time crawling around on the ground, but they can fly when they have to. They fly to escape from danger or look for food.

Ladybugs have two pairs of wings. The front pair are hard wing cases. These protect the back pair, which are folded out of sight when not in use.

A ladybug prepares for flight.

❶ Before take-off, a ladybug crawls to the top of a stem. ▶

◀ **❷** The ladybug opens its hard wing cases.

❸ It unfolds its delicate flying wings and beats them up and down. ▶

◀ **❹** Soon the wings beat so quickly that they lift the ladybug into the air.

Laying Eggs

Like many insects, a ladybug goes through four different stages as it grows. This is called its life cycle. The first stage of its life cycle is an egg.

▲

❶ *Male and female ladybugs mate in the warm days of spring and summer.*

◀ **❷** *About a week later, the female lays her eggs on a plant where there are plenty of aphids.*

About a week after they are laid, the eggs change color. They are ready to hatch. The thin shells begin to split, and wriggly creatures called larvae crawl out. The larva is the second stage of a ladybug's life cycle.

❸ *The tiny yellow eggs stand up like bowling pins. There are about twenty-five eggs in a batch.*

❹ *All the eggs hatch at the same time. The tiny larvae twist and turn until they get free of the shell.*

▼

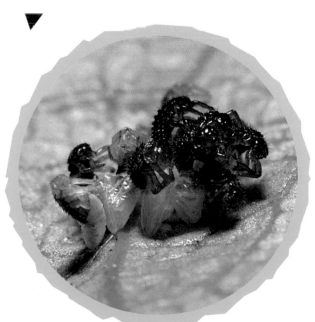

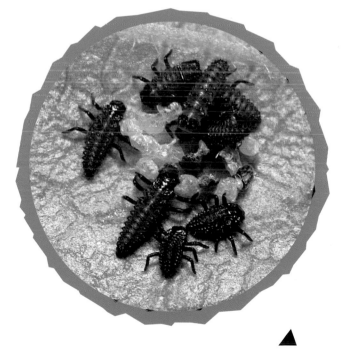

❺ *Once the larvae have hatched, their first meal is the egg shell.* ▲

Life as a Larva

A ladybug larva looks nothing like its parents. It has a long, thin body made up of segments, which are covered with tiny bristles. It has three pairs of legs like an adult ladybug, but it has no wings and cannot fly.

Ladybug larvae feed on aphids, just like their parents do. They eat so much that they grow very quickly. They are soon too big for their skin. The old skin splits open and the larva wriggles out. It has a new skin with room to grow.

This larva is hunting for food. It eats about thirty aphids every day.

Becoming an Adult

About three weeks after hatching from its egg, a larva is fully grown. It stops feeding and glues itself to a plant. Now it will become a pupa. This is the third stage in a ladybug's life cycle.

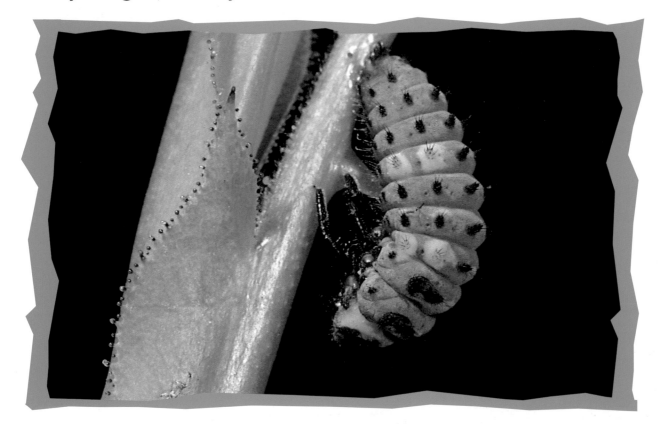

A larva sticks itself to a plant before becoming a pupa.

From pupa to ladybug

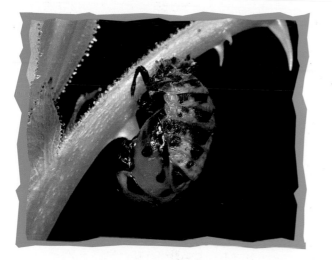

❶ The larva has shed its skin for the last time and is turning into a pupa. Inside the pupa, the insect's body begins to change.

❷ About a week later, the pupa splits open, and an adult ladybug crawls out.

❸ A ladybug's wing cases are yellow at first. The red color and spots appear after about a day.

Staying Alive

Ladybugs have a smart way of staying alive. They smell and taste very bad. Most animals that try to eat ladybugs spit

them out. This is a lesson the animal never forgets. When it sees beetles with red wing cases, it leaves them alone!

A ladybug's spots and bright colors are a warning that it tastes very bad.

When a ladybug is frightened, a bitter, yellow juice oozes out of its legs. This scares the enemy away.

◀ Ladybugs still have some enemies. This ladybug is being attacked by a shieldbug.

If a ladybug is attacked, it defends itself by biting the enemy with a nasty-tasting poison. It might even roll over and pretend to be dead.

In a Swarm

Ladybugs sometimes gather in large groups called swarms and fly off somewhere new. They do this when there are too many of them in one place and food is running out. Spreading out helps them survive.

A swarm of ladybugs spreads out to look for food.

Some swarms fly very long distances.
Every summer, millions of ladybugs in
California fly 50 miles to escape from
the heat of the valleys. They fly
back the following spring.

A Winter Sleep

Some ladybugs hibernate in the winter. The weather is too cold, and there are no aphids to eat. The ladybugs huddle under the bark of a tree or hide in attics and sheds.

Some kinds of ladybugs spend the winter in the same places year after year.

A ladybug hibernates in the bark of a tree during the winter.

Sometimes millions of ladybugs squeeze together and hibernate under the snow. Their bodies have a special chemical that keeps them from freezing to death.

When the snow melts in spring, the ladybugs fly off to mate and look for food.

A blanket of snow protects ladybugs from the cold winter air.

The Gardener's Friend

Ladybugs are a great help to gardeners and farmers. They feed on pests that eat plants and crops. With the ladybugs' help, growers do not need chemicals to protect their crops. This is good for the food people eat and good for the soil, too.

Ladybugs help get rid of pests without using chemical sprays.

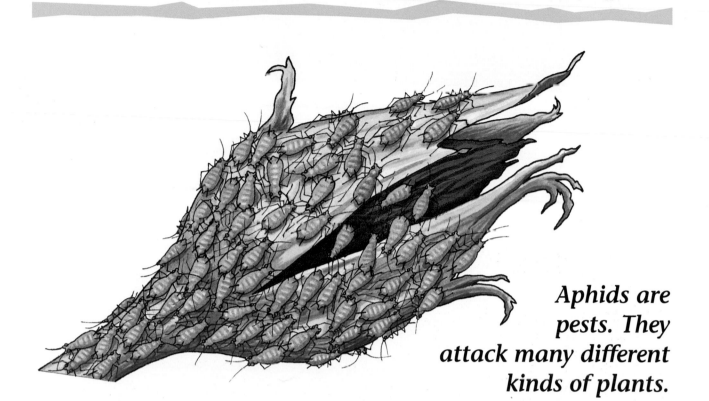

Aphids are pests. They attack many different kinds of plants.

In some parts of the world, farmers buy ladybugs and larvae to spread around their fields. They hope the insects will protect their plants and help them harvest extra crops.

Some growers buy ladybugs to protect their plants.

Ladybug Life!

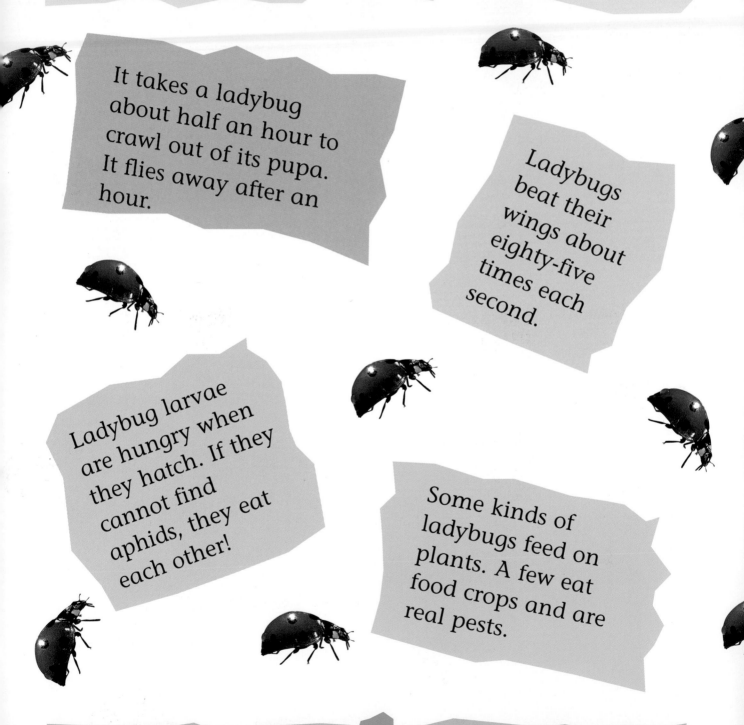

It takes a ladybug about half an hour to crawl out of its pupa. It flies away after an hour.

Ladybugs beat their wings about eighty-five times each second.

Ladybug larvae are hungry when they hatch. If they cannot find aphids, they eat each other!

Some kinds of ladybugs feed on plants. A few eat food crops and are real pests.

"Ladybug, ladybug, fly away home. Your house is on fire and your children all gone." People said this rhyme long ago after the harvest, when farmers set fire to their fields.

People used to think ladybugs were a cure for toothache, measles, and tummy ache.

There are over four thousand different kinds of ladybugs.

In Britain, ladybugs are known as ladybirds.

A female ladybug lays about four hundred eggs in her lifetime.

The life cycle of a ladybug only takes four weeks. Ladybugs born in May can be great-grandparents by August!

Glossary

abdomen	the last of the three parts of an insect's body
antenna	one of the two feelers on a ladybug's head (plural: antennae)
beetles	a group of insects that have hard wing cases and can usually fly
exoskeleton	the hard outer coat that protects the body of insects and other small animals
larva	the young stage of an insect after it hatches out of an egg (plural: larvae)
life cycle	the different stages that an animal goes through in life
pupa	the stage in an insect's life when it changes from a larva to an adult (plural: pupae)
thorax	the middle part of an insect's body, in between the head and the abdomen

Index